Camino de Santiago Guidebook
A Travel Guide to Planning Your Ideal Pilgrimage to St. James

by

OV Travel Publishing

TABLE OF CONTENTS

"Going on from there, he saw two other brothers, James son of Zebedee and his brother John. They were in a boat with their father Zebedee, preparing their nets. Jesus called them, and immediately they left the boat and their father and followed him."

Matthew 4: 21-22

HERE YOUR FIRST BONUS!

Dear reader and fellow pilgrim,

I want to start by expressing my gratitude for choosing to trust this guide. I am confident it will meet your expectations as it accompanies you from the early stages of planning all the way to the moment you reach your final destination.

The biblical verse referenced here speaks of James, the very same James whose remains, according to Christian tradition, have rested in Santiago de Compostela for over a thousand years. This passage illustrates how James, when called by Jesus, left everything behind to follow Him. I believe that even today, the Camino de Santiago "calls" to each pilgrim who decides to embark on this journey, much like Jesus called the one who would become an apostle.

This will be a journey filled with excitement, offering diverse experiences, breathtaking landscapes, historic sites, camaraderie among fellow pilgrims, and profound spiritual moments.

To show my appreciation for your trust, I want to begin by offering you an initial bonus, which I'm certain will be useful to you throughout your Camino (especially at the end of each day).

This bonus addresses one of the key aspects of the journey: your accommodations. During my own pilgrimages, I often found myself without reliable information on which hotels, hostels or "albergues" to choose, or even where to locate them. For this reason, I've decided to share a link to the most up-to-date website on this topic, which provides information on the various options available for each route and stage of your journey.

My suggestion is to take a screenshot of the different options each morning before you set out, so that even if you lose internet access, you'll still have everything you need in your photo gallery.

You can scan the QR code below to access it. Until we meet again, fellow traveler, I wish you a happy reading experience!

CHAPTER 1: A CALL THROUGH TIME

SANTIAGO DE COMPOSTELA
ST JAMES OF COMPOSTELLA

THE HISTORY OF THE "CAMINO DE SANTIAGO"

The Ancient Origins of The Journey

The Way of St. James, enveloped in the timeless mystique of centuries past, is far more than just a path; it is a journey rich with history, faith and mystery, unfolding across the fabric of time itself. Imagine the "Camino" as an ancient manuscript, with its first lines inscribed at the dawn of history, written with the ink of heroic endeavors and legendary feats.

We are transported back to the 9th century, a time when the news of the Apostle James's remains being discovered in Santiago de Compostela began to circulate. In a medieval world steeped in faith and woven with legends, a path emerged, threading like a golden strand through the wild and majestic landscapes of northern Spain.

This path, born out of deep faith and driven by human curiosity, weaves like a crimson thread through the history of Europe. It winds through ancient woodlands, medieval cities and towns with evocative names, each holding stories carved into their stones and soil. The stars that guided the first pilgrims continue to light the night sky, and the call of the Camino echoes through the ages, drawing those who seek to connect with their innermost selves.

This pilgrimage is far more than a mere route; it is a journey into the heart of humanity, a narrative written in the hearts of those brave enough to tread this ancient path. With each step, we feel the echoes of centuries of pilgrims shaping this route and our own destiny. As we begin our journey, we become part of an eternal story, woven into the epic history of the "Camino de Santiago".

The Historical and Spiritual Accounts

The Way of St. James unfolds as a vibrant mosaic of accounts, turning pilgrims into narrators of ancient and untold stories. Anne, as she crosses the plains of Burgos, feels the stones underfoot as reservoirs of countless experiences. She writes in her journal, "As I walk, I feel the steps of those who traversed this path centuries before me".

As we delve into history, we meet Javier, a passionate researcher deciphering ancient codes within the cathedrals along the Camino. Through his perspective, these grand structures are seen not just as stones meticulously arranged, but as poetic expressions in stone, telling tales of faith and devotion. During a serendipitous meeting in León, pilgrims from different corners of the globe share their stories. Carlos, a doctor from Argentina, speaks of how the Camino helped him heal emotional wounds, while Emma, an artist from Australia, found creative inspiration in the Gothic cathedrals.

These testimonies are not only spoken; they are etched into the walls of monasteries and written in the diaries of travelers. When pilgrims like us pause to reflect at the ancient Iron Cross, they can sense the weight of hopes and dreams left by those who came before. These stories form the background melody of our pilgrimage, a constant call to deepen our connection with history and spirituality. Through these accounts, the Camino becomes a dialogue between those who set out centuries ago and those who continue the journey today, a timeless symphony of steps woven into the grand tapestry of pilgrimage.

The Cultural and Religious Significance

Immersed in the spirit of the Camino de Santiago, a realm of cultural and religious significance unfolds like an ancient scroll through the pages of time. It is a story of faith interwoven with golden threads of age-old traditions and reverence.

As one walks on the stones that have endured for millennia, the sacred seems to pulse beneath the surface, as though the earth itself recounts the tales of those who walked upon it in pursuit of spirituality. The cathedrals, grand and ethereal, stand as guardians of the link between the earthly and the divine, symbols that transcend the limits of language.

A living metaphor of this connection lies in the ancient legend of the scallop shells of Santiago. Every pilgrim, symbolized by the shell attached to their backpack, becomes part of a millennial narrative. The shell is more than just a travel emblem; it is an icon that unites souls in a collective spiritual journey.

In the heart of the cities along the route, such as Pamplona with its ancient fortifications, one discovers that the "Camino" is a resonance of history. Every step is an act of respect for those who, over centuries, embarked on the same journey, a celebration that unfolds through cobbled streets and tree-lined plazas.

The light of faith also shines in the most secluded places; as one crosses silent woods and green valleys, the ancient breath of hidden sanctuaries can be felt among the trees. A hermitage, hidden like a secret guarded by nature, becomes a haven for those seeking a deeper connection with the divine.

Encounters with people of various faiths and backgrounds reveal the diversity of beliefs intertwined in a shared tapestry of mutual respect. The Camino becomes a crossroads where differences blend into a shared pursuit of something greater than ourselves.

In this spiritual epic, cultural and religious significance serve as the binding force that unites travelers in a timeless dance. Each chapter of the Camino is a page in this ancient book, and the pilgrim becomes the author of a story written with every step taken.

SIGNIFICANT STATISTICS AND INSIGHTS

Nationality, Age, Gender, and Participation Patterns of the Most Popular Routes

The Camino de Santiago is a rich tapestry of interconnected stories, with each pilgrim adding a unique thread to the global mosaic. Statistics serve as our lens to closely examine this diverse human experience.

Nationalities:
The Camino is like a cultural runway where nationalities merge as colors on a painter's canvas. Pilgrims from Italy, Germany, the United States and numerous other countries embark on this shared spiritual journey, though the majority of participants are of Spanish origin.

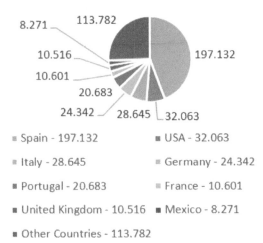

- Spain - 197.132
- USA - 32.063
- Italy - 28.645
- Germany - 24.342
- Portugal - 20.683
- France - 10.601
- United Kingdom - 10.516
- Mexico - 8.271
- Other Countries - 113.782

Age:

On the Camino, age maps the passage of time. From eager young adventurers in search of new experiences to more seasoned souls seeking introspection, each step contributes a distinctive chapter to the pilgrimage's ongoing story. Pilgrims' ages typically range from 18 to 65, though some travelers fall outside these bounds, either younger or older.

Gender:

The statistics reveal an intriguing balance, with women making up 52% of pilgrims and men 48%. The Camino thus becomes a path of connection and exploration for people of all genders.

Participation Patterns:

The seasons dictate the ebb and flow of the Camino, with peak attendance occurring between May and October. During these months, the trails bustle with the determined footsteps of pilgrims, creating a lively and warm atmosphere. The journey, however, often begins in April, marking the transition from the quieter low season to the more bustling high season.

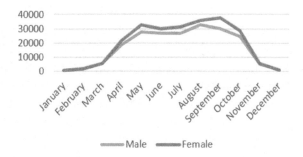

Most Popular Routes:
Amidst the vast array of routes, certain ones stand out. The French Way is particularly favored by beginners, offering well-developed infrastructure and services. The Northern Way, more demanding, traces the coast through cities such as San Sebastian, Bilbao and Santander. The Primitive Way, with its challenging elevations, winds through awe-inspiring landscapes. The English Way, a shorter alternative, presents a unique perspective beginning from La Coruna.

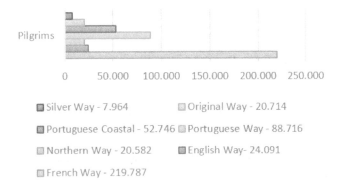

These statistics provide the backdrop for the narrative of the Camino, enriching the experience with layers of meaning beyond mere numbers. Through these figures, pilgrims can see themselves as part of a global fellowship, united by the enduring allure of Santiago de Compostela.

CHAPTER 2: PREPARE YOUR SPIRIT….AND YOUR BACKPACK

MOTIVATIONS AND EXPECTATIONS

Dear Pilgrim, what are you up to at this very moment?

Are you mapping out your stages? Or maybe you're already packing your suitcase? Perhaps you're already soaking in the stunning landscapes that the Camino offers?

No matter where you are in your journey, I'm sure you're experiencing a whirlwind of emotions because that's exactly what the Camino stirs within us. It doesn't matter whether your motivation is rooted in a spiritual quest to embark on an inner journey that promises self-discovery. Or maybe your drive is sparked by a hunger for adventure, eager to wander through scenic landscapes and immerse yourself in the magic of cities like Pamplona, Leon and Burgos.

I hope that, like me, you're brimming with enthusiasm, ready to embrace this journey with immense joy and a desire to savor every step. Because this experience is, above all, a collection of emotions, encounters with yourself and with fellow pilgrims. It's about sunrises that paint the sky with golden hues and nights under a star-filled sky that gently cradles you like an ancient melody.

So, I won't keep you any longer, allowing you to dream about the sights and feelings that await you on your journey.

As for us, we're prepared, with this guide, to walk alongside you, to explore the emotional landscape of your journey together. We aim to equip you with everything you need to navigate this experience, and to be there for you, both in the beautiful moments and in those times when you might need a little extra support.

THE PILGRIM'S CREDENTIAL

Significance and Acquisition

What exactly is the Pilgrim's Credential?

The Credential is far more than just a document; it is the very heartbeat of the Camino de Santiago. It serves as a spiritual passport, chronicling the stages completed and the encounters made along the way.

Its origins stretch back centuries, when pilgrims, upon reaching the tomb of Saint James, would provide proof of their journey. Initially, these proofs were verbal testimonies or mementos gathered along the route. However, as time passed, the need for an official document became apparent.

Thus, the Credential, also known as the "Pilgrim's Passport" or "Pilgrim's Accreditation", was introduced to formally document the pilgrim's progress. This crucial document can be obtained from various places, including the International Pilgrim Welcome Centre, offices of pilgrim confraternities, hostels, parish churches and associations of friends of the Way of St. James around the world (with proof of identity). Each stage of the journey is marked with a stamp, recording the pilgrim's path along the Camino. It is a personal, unique and irreplaceable document, filled with stamps from churches, hostels and other significant spots along the way.

But the Credential is more than just a practical document; it symbolizes community and shared experience. Every pilgrim carries a blank Credential, ready to be filled with memories from their journey. Along the way, a special bond forms between pilgrims and those who issue the stamps. It's a moment of connection, where the pilgrim is

13

welcomed and acknowledged in their quest.

There's an interesting anecdote about the oldest Credentials, carefully preserved by pilgrims over the centuries. Some of these bear the marks of wear and tear, tangible evidence of the challenges faced along the way. These ancient documents are like fragments of pilgrimage stories, each one holding its own unique significance.

The Credential is not just a piece of paper; it's a journey unto itself. It's the medium through which the stories of pilgrims are interwoven with those who walked before them. It embodies the commitment, perseverance and spirituality of the pilgrim.

Ultimately, obtaining the Credential is not merely a bureaucratic step but a meaningful ritual that marks the pilgrim's entry into an age-old community of spiritual travelers.

Purpose and connection with Compostela

Let's now delve into the significance of the Credential, your indispensable companion on the famed Camino de Santiago. While it's important to note that carrying the Credential is not mandatory to walk the Camino, its value becomes increasingly evident as the journey unfolds, particularly for those who aspire to receive the coveted "Compostela".

The main purpose of the Credential is to serve as a symbolic testament to your spiritual journey; each stamp you collect along the way not only marks your physical progress but also captures the essence of the pilgrimage itself: a blend of spiritual discovery, personal challenges and communal bonds.

As you near the end of your pilgrimage in Santiago de Compostela, the Credential takes on an even more vital role. To receive the Compostela, a certificate acknowledging the completion of your pilgrimage, you must present your Credential, filled with the stamps gathered throughout your journey.

The Compostela, typically issued by the International Pilgrim Welcome Centre located at Rúa Carretas number 33, is awarded to pilgrims who have traveled at least 100 km on foot or horseback, or 200 km by bicycle. It is more than just a certificate; it is a testament, a "visual diary" that reflects the pilgrim's dedication, endurance and spiritual journey.

The Pilgrim's Credential transforms from a simple document into a narrative thread that weaves together the physical and spiritual dimensions of the Camino de Santiago. Its story does not end with the final stamp; it continues seamlessly within the sacred walls of the Cathedral, where the Compostela awaits you!

ITEMS TO PACK AND TO LEAVE BEHIND

We've already discussed how thrilling the Camino de Santiago can be, but it's also essential to recognize that it can be quite demanding, both physically and mentally. Knowing what to pack and what to leave out can make a significant difference in ensuring your journey is smoother and less problematic. In this chapter, we'll go over everything you'll need, starting with the essentials.

Items to Pack:

Backpack with rain cover (35 to 50 liters max): This is crucial for comfortably carrying all your belongings; the rain cover will protect your gear in case of unexpected weather.

Hiking shoes: Invest in sturdy, comfortable footwear suitable for the terrain. Hiking shoes will provide the necessary support and protection for those long treks.

Sleeping bag (or a sheet bag for July and August): Especially useful in hostels, make sure you have the right gear to ensure a restful sleep.

Water bottle, small bottles or a camel bag: Staying hydrated is key. Bring lightweight, reusable containers for water.

Headlamp: Essential for early morning starts or for finding your way in dark hostels.

Appropriate clothing: This includes a fleece or sweater, a wind jacket and/or poncho, hiking pants, short-sleeved technical shirts, underwear, technical socks, sweatpants and a long-sleeved shirt for sleeping. Be prepared for unpredictable weather by packing versatile clothing.

Tissues or wipes in abundance: Handy for maintaining personal hygiene throughout your journey.

Microfiber towels: Bring one small and one large for daily use.

Wide-brimmed hat or cap: Protect your head from the sun, particularly during the summer months.

Personal hygiene kit: Carry the basics for personal care, including deodorant, toothbrush, toothpaste and other essentials.

First aid kit: Include an anti-inflammatory ointment, bandages, plasters, disinfectant, needles, cotton thread, a few paracetamol pills or sachets, anti-inflammatory medication and any necessary personal prescriptions.

Wallet with documents: Ensure you have your ID, money, ATM card, credit or prepaid card and health insurance card.

Earplugs: Useful for getting a good night's sleep in shared hostels.

Shower sandals: For hygiene and comfort during your stays at hostels.

Marseille soap: A versatile soap, great for both personal use and washing clothes.

Smartphone, charger (preferably with multiple USB ports), earphones: Handy for navigation, staying in touch and entertainment during downtime.

And don't forget, as we've discussed earlier, if you want to receive the Compostela, remember to bring **your Credential**.

Oh, and one more thing: don't forget to take this guide with you; it's sure to be a great help along the way! 😊

Items to Consider:

Trekking Poles: While not absolutely necessary, trekking poles can help reduce knee strain on descents and provide additional support on tougher terrain. Consider whether including them suits your personal preferences.

Thermal Jacket or Extra Fleece: Temperatures can fluctuate significantly during the Camino. Think about whether you might need an extra layer to keep warm.

Backpack with Hydration System: Although this was mentioned as a "recommended option" earlier, we're highlighting it here since not everyone may consider it. Some pilgrims prefer backpacks equipped with integrated hydration systems, like a camel bag. Assess if this feature aligns better with your needs.

Rain Cover for the Backpack: If your backpack's built-in rain cover isn't sufficient, it might be worth investing in a separate cover to ensure your gear stays fully protected.

GPS Navigation Device or App: While the Camino's stages are well-marked, some pilgrims like the reassurance of a navigation device to avoid getting lost. Consider whether a dedicated GPS or a Camino-specific app would be beneficial for you.

Trash Bag: Even though the trails are equipped with trash bins, it's important to respect the environment.

Consider carrying a small trash bag with you to help keep the Camino clean.

Extra Snacks and Water: Think about whether you'll need to carry additional food and water, particularly on longer stages or in less populated areas.

Compressible Travel Pillow: If you're seeking extra comfort while sleeping in hostels, you might want to consider bringing a compressible pillow.

Reflective Coat or Vest: Increase your visibility, especially if you anticipate walking during low-light conditions.

Noise-Canceling Earphones: Consider the benefits of noise-canceling earphones for resting peacefully in potentially noisy environments.

Power Bank: Make sure you have sufficient battery power for your smartphone and other electronic devices during your journey. Choose a power bank with the capacity that meets your needs.

Items to Leave Behind:

Excessive Weight in the Backpack: Steer clear of overloading your backpack with non-essential items. Keeping it light will make for a more comfortable and less tiring walk.

Inappropriate Footwear: Avoid bringing shoes that are either new or unsuitable for trekking. Ensure that you have comfortable, well-broken-in footwear before starting the Camino.

Too Much Clothing: Refrain from packing an excess of

clothes. Opt for versatile items that can adapt to varying weather conditions.

Unnecessary Valuables: Leave behind any valuables that aren't essential for the Camino. Minimize carrying expensive jewelry or items that could easily be lost or damaged.

Heavy and Bulky Clothes: Avoid packing clothes that take up too much space. Choose items that are lightweight and compact.

Overreliance on Technology: Don't depend entirely on technology for navigation. Batteries can deplete and devices can fail. Maintain some self-reliance and develop basic navigation skills.

Disposable Plastic Bags: Try to limit the use of disposable plastics. Bring a reusable water bottle and do your part to reduce plastic waste along the Camino.

A Few Tips on What to Avoid Emotionally:

Overplanning: Avoid meticulously planning every aspect of your trip; leave room for spontaneity and unexpected moments along the way.

Rushing: Don't walk too fast. The Camino is meant to be savored, so take your time to fully appreciate the spiritual and natural aspects of the journey.

Now, you're ready to embark on your adventure!

Download the Maps by scanning here:

CHAPTER 3: ENCHANTING ROUTES AND VARIOUS WAYS TO TRAVEL

THE FRENCH WAY

Characteristics, Practical Advice and Stages

Dear Pilgrim, the French Way, spanning roughly 781 km, is a captivating route brimming with unforgettable experiences. It stands out as the most popular and well-supported paths on the Camino de  Santiago. In this section, I'll walk you through its main characteristics and offer practical tips to ensure your journey is a success.

One of the most engaging aspects of the Camino Francés is the extensive network of accommodations and services available along the way. You'll encounter a variety of landscapes, from forested trails to charming valleys, offering stunning views of the French countryside.

Physical and Mental Preparation:

Embarking on this journey requires both physical endurance and mental fortitude. It's a good idea to begin a training regimen that includes long, varied walks. Additionally, work on building your mental toughness, which will be crucial when dealing with inclines and fatigue.

Timing and Weather:

The ideal time to walk the Camino Francés is between May and October, with the busiest period falling between June and September. However, be ready for changing weather conditions. Pack clothing that accommodates different temperatures and bring a waterproof poncho for sudden rain showers.

Navigation and Signage:
The Camino Francés is generally well-marked with arrows and symbols to guide you along the way, but having a detailed map can be useful for better orientation. Keep an eye on the signs and don't hesitate to ask for directions if needed.

Starting Points, Stages and Distances:

The French Way typically begins either in Saint-Jean-Pied-de-Port or Roncesvalles. If your journey starts in Saint-Jean-Pied-de-Port, keep reading:

From Saint-Jean-Pied-de-Port to Roncesvalles:

Starting from here, you'll traverse the Pyrenees and arrive in Roncesvalles, Spain, covering approximately 25 km. This opening segment offers stunning vistas but can be demanding due to the mountain crossing.
Difficulty: Moderate.

If your adventure begins in Roncesvalles, read on from here:

From Roncesvalles to Zubiri:

The next stage guides you through enchanting woodlands and charming villages. Zubiri, located about 22 km from Roncesvalles, serves as your resting place after an engaging day.
Difficulty: Easy/Moderate.

From Zubiri to Pamplona:

As you head towards Pamplona, roughly 20 km away, you'll pass through this historic city, known for its old town and Plaza de Toros, offering a great chance to dive into

Spanish culture.
Difficulty: Easy.

From Pamplona to Puente la Reina:

Departing from Pamplona, you'll journey towards Puente la Reina, traversing rural landscapes. This stage is about 24 km long, passing ancient bridges and small villages, with some challenging terrain despite the well-marked path.
Difficulty: Moderate.

From Puente la Reina to Estella:

This 22 km stage takes you through golden fields and rolling green hills, leading to Estella, a city steeped in history and culture.
Difficulty: Moderate.

From Estella to Los Arcos:

This stage, about 21 km long, guides you to Los Arcos through wheat fields and rural landscapes that encapsulate the essence of the Camino.
Difficulty: Easy.

From Los Arcos to Logroño:

As you walk through vineyards and farmlands, you'll reach Logroño, a city renowned for its wines. This 27 km stage allows you to savor the beauty of La Rioja's wine country.
Difficulty: Easy.

From Logroño to Nájera:

You'll cover around 30 km, passing through hills and forests before arriving in Nájera, offering a comprehensive experience of Spain's varied landscapes.

Difficulty: Moderate.

From Nájera to Santo Domingo de la Calzada:

This 21 km stage leads you to Santo Domingo de la Calzada, a city rich in history with an impressive cathedral.

Difficulty: Easy.

From Santo Domingo de la Calzada to Belorado:

Covering about 22 km, you'll reach Belorado, traveling through quaint villages and the picturesque Spanish countryside.

Difficulty: Easy.

From Belorado to Burgos:

The journey to Burgos, about 30 km long, takes you through forests and open fields, concluding at the magnificent Burgos Cathedral.

Difficulty: Moderate, due to its length.

From Burgos to Hontanas:

Leaving the grandeur of Burgos behind, your next stop is Hontanas, roughly 30 km away. Along the route, you'll appreciate the beauty of the Meseta, a vast and expansive plain.

Difficulty: Moderate, due to its length.

From Hontanas to Boadilla del Camino:

Walking approximately 30 km, you'll arrive in Boadilla del Camino. This stage crosses golden fields and small villages, offering an authentic glimpse into rural Spanish life.

Difficulty: Moderate, due to its length.

From Boadilla del Camino to Carrión de los Condes:

Your journey continues with a stage of about 28 km leading to Carrión de los Condes. Along the way, you'll cross the famous Canal de Castilla and enjoy extraordinarily beautiful landscapes.
Difficulty: Moderate.

From Carrion de los Condes to Terradillos de los Templarios:

Leaving Carrión de los Condes, you'll cover roughly 26 km to reach Terradillos de los Templarios. This stretch will immerse you in the peacefulness and serenity of the countryside.
Difficulty: Easy.

From Terradillos de los Templarios to Bercianos del Real Camino:

Your next stop, approximately 23 km away, is Bercianos del Real Camino. This stage takes you across expansive open fields, allowing you to retrace some of the steps from earlier in your journey.
Difficulty: Easy.

From Bercianos del Real Camino to Mansilla de las Mulas:

After walking about 27 km, you'll arrive in Mansilla de las Mulas, following rural paths and passing through small villages along the way.
Difficulty: Moderate, due to a few more demanding sections.

From Mansilla de las Mulas to León:

Your next major stop is the city of León, with a stage of around 19 km. Here, you'll have the opportunity to delve into the rich history and architecture of this enchanting city.
Difficulty: Easy.

From León to Hospital de Órbigo:

Continuing from León, your journey will take you to Hospital de Órbigo, a stage of about 31 km. This segment presents a variety of landscapes, transitioning from urban streets to natural trails.
Difficulty: Moderate, due to some slightly tougher stretches.

From Hospital de Órbigo to Astorga:

With a stage of approximately 17 km, you'll reach Astorga, known for its stunning architecture and the Episcopal Palace designed by Antoni Gaudí.
Difficulty: Easy.

*From Astorga to Rabanal del Camino:

Your journey continues with a stage of about 20 km to Rabanal del Camino, a welcoming village set amidst beautiful natural surroundings.
Difficulty: Moderate, due to some gentle inclines.

From Rabanal del Camino to Ponferrada:

After covering roughly 32 km, you'll arrive in Ponferrada, home to the impressive and historic Templar Castle.
Difficulty: Moderate, due to some challenging elevations.

From Ponferrada to Villafranca del Bierzo:

With a stage of about 24 km, you'll reach Villafranca del Bierzo, a town that still retains much of its medieval charm.
Difficulty: Easy.

From Villafranca del Bierzo to O Cebreiro:

This stage, about 27 km in length, begins your ascent into the heights, offering breathtaking views as you approach O Cebreiro.
Difficulty: Challenging.

From O Cebreiro to Triacastela:

In this 21 km stage, you'll make your way to Triacastela, traversing woodlands and rolling green hills.
Difficulty: Moderate, due to the slightly more demanding terrain.

From Triacastela to Sarria:

Sarria, situated about 18 km away, will be your next destination. This stage takes you through charming villages and picturesque green landscapes.
Difficulty: Easy.

From Sarria to Portomarín:

From Sarria, you'll walk about 23 km to Portomarín, crossing the Miño River and exploring this historic town.
Difficulty: Moderate.

From Portomarín to Palas de Rei:

Continuing your journey, you'll travel roughly 25 km to Palas de Rei, following wooded paths and countryside trails. Difficulty: Moderate.

From Palas de Rei to Arzúa:

After walking approximately 29 km, you'll reach Arzúa, surrounded by the natural beauty of Galicia.
Difficulty: Easy.

*From Arzúa to O Pedrouzo:

This stage, about 19 km in length, will take you to O Pedrouzo, bringing you ever closer to your final destination. Difficulty: Easy.

From O Pedrouzo to Santiago de Compostela:

Your final stage, spanning about 20 km, will lead you to Santiago de Compostela, where you'll be greeted by the magnificent Cathedral, marking the end of your extraordinary journey.
Difficulty: Easy.

Interest Places (Cathedrals, Museums) and Iconic Landmarks

Now, we arrive at the key sites worth visiting along your journey, provided you have the time and energy.

Of course, this is not an exhaustive list: there are countless attractions you could explore along such a long and extensive route. However, we wanted to offer a few recommendations for spots we believe you absolutely shouldn't miss!

Saint-Jean-Pied-de-Port:

Begin your pilgrimage in Saint-Jean-Pied-de-Port, a charming French town that serves as a starting point for many pilgrims. The town's Saint-Jean-Baptiste Cathedral is a 13th-century architectural marvel. Its impressive towers and detailed façade are testaments to the artistry of the period. Legend says that pilgrims who touch the famous Notre-Dame Cloister before setting out will be protected throughout their journey.

Pamplona:

Pamplona, renowned for its Running of the Bulls, is also home to historical sites like the Pamplona Cathedral. The cathedral's peaceful cloister and Gothic  architecture offer a striking contrast to the city's lively festivities.

Burgos:

As you continue towards Burgos, make sure to visit the
Cathedral of Santa
Maria (image), a
UNESCO World
Heritage site. This grand
Gothic cathedral houses
the tomb of El Cid, the
legend ary hero and

knight. The annual "Nazarine Episode," a religious drama
from the 15th century, is performed here. Another
fascinating stop in Burgos is the Museum of Human
Evolution, which showcases unique archaeological finds
that delve into the story of human evolution.

León:

In León, the Cathedral of
Santa Mari a is a breathtaking
sight, famous for its stunning
stained-glass windows and the
magnificent Judgment Gate.
Nearby, the Basilica of San
Isidoro, with its Royal

Pantheon, tells the history of the Spanish monarchy. Don't
miss the Casa Botines (image), a modernist masterpiece
designed by Antoni Gaudí.

Astorga:

Astorga boasts the Episcopal Palace, another Gaudí
masterpiece that blends Gothic and Moorish influences.
Also, be sure to explore the Roman Museum, where
archaeological discoveries offer insights into Astorga's
Roman past. The streets of Astorga are rich with stories of
pilgrims and their journeys through the ages.

Sarria:

In Sarria, the Church of Santa Mariña offers a peaceful place for reflection. This town is a significant starting point for many pilgrims aiming to earn the Compostela, as it lies less than 100 km from Santiago.

Santiago de Compostela:

Your journey culminates at the Santiago de Compostela Cathedral (image). Pilgrims gather in Obradoiro Square to admire the cathedral's stunning façade. The interior is equally awe-inspiring, with the Holy Sepulcher Shrine and the reliquary of the apostle James. The "Botafumeiro," the massive censer, adds a mystical element to the solemn masses.

THE NORTHERN WAY

Characteristics, Practical Advice and Stages

Dear Pilgrim, the Northern Way, stretching approximately 825 km, offers a truly unique experience as it takes you through stunning coastal landscapes and charming communities.

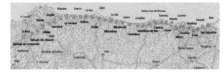

Here are some key highlights and practical advice to help you successfully navigate the Northern Way.

Physical and Mental Preparation:
Proper physical conditioning is crucial for handling the varied challenges of the Northern Way. Begin a training regimen that includes long walks and cardiovascular exercises; given the diverse terrain, mental preparedness is also essential. You'll need stamina and determination to endure long days and unpredictable weather conditions.

Timing and Weather:
The Northern Way is known for its variable coastal weather. The ideal time to embark on this journey is between May and September, when you can avoid the harshness of winter. However, be ready for sudden changes in the weather. Pack clothing that is versatile and suitable for both sunny and rainy conditions.

Nutrition and Hydration:
Maintaining good nutrition and staying hydrated are vital throughout your journey. Carry energy-boosting snacks and a reusable water bottle. Along the way, you'll also have the chance to enjoy the local cuisine, so don't miss the opportunity to indulge in some regional specialties.

Navigation and Signage:

The signage along the Northern Way is generally well-maintained, but it's always a good idea to carry a detailed map. Pay close attention to the signs, and if you're ever uncertain, don't hesitate to ask locals for directions. While the coastal views are breathtaking, be prepared for potential detours due to weather changes or roadworks.

Starting Points, Stages and Distances:

From Irún to San Sebastián:

Starting your journey from Irún, the first stage takes you to San Sebastián, passing through a mix of coastal and urban landscapes. You'll cover approximately 25 km, enjoying sweeping views of the Cantabrian Sea along the way. Though challenging, the stage rewards you with stunning panoramas.
Difficulty: Moderate.

From San Sebastián to Zarautz:

Leaving San Sebastián, the next stage leads you to Zarautz, spanning about 22 km. This section of the route takes you along the Basque coast, with paths that traverse beaches and hilly terrain. The landscape is varied, offering a mix of easier sections and some that are slightly more demanding.
Difficulty: Moderate.

From Zarautz to Deba:

Continuing along the coastline, the stage from Zarautz to Deba covers around 21 km. You'll walk through picturesque coastal areas and charming villages. This stretch is relatively easy and suitable for walkers of all levels.
Difficulty: Easy.

From Deba to Markina-Xemein:

The next leg of the journey takes you from Deba to Markina-Xemein, covering a distance of about 22 km. The route winds through hilly and wooded areas, offering diverse and scenic views. While the terrain can be somewhat challenging, the natural beauty of the path makes the effort worthwhile.

Difficulty: Moderate.

From Markina-Xemein to Gernika-Lumo:

As you continue toward Gernika-Lumo, you'll travel approximately 20 km through hilly and rural landscapes. The terrain is varied but generally manageable, providing an authentic glimpse of the Basque countryside.

Difficulty: Easy.

From Gernika-Lumo to Lezama:

The following stage takes you from Gernika-Lumo to Lezama, covering roughly 27 km. This route passes through open countryside within the Basque region, including the Urdaibai Biosphere Reserve, a uniquely scenic and protected area.

Difficulty: Moderate.

From Lezama to Bilbao:

Starting from Lezama, you'll reach Bilbao after about 11 km. This final stretch is relatively short, taking you through some notable attractions that we'll explore in the next section. The walk is straightforward and suitable for walkers of all skill levels.

Difficulty: Easy.

From Bilbao to Portugalete:

After Bilbao, the next stage takes you to Portugalete, spanning approximately 19 km. This stage crosses urban areas and riverside landscapes, offering a unique view of the famous Puente Colgante (Hanging Bridge).
Difficulty: Easy.

From Portugalete to Castro-Urdiales:

Continuing along the coast, you'll reach Castro-Urdiales after walking about 27.5 km. Along this stretch, you'll traverse old railroad tracks that once carried iron from local villages.
Difficulty: Moderate.

From Castro-Urdiales to Laredo:

Following the coastline, your journey will take you to Laredo, covering roughly 26.5 km. This stage offers stunning coastal views, though some sections may pose a challenge.
Difficulty: Moderate.

From Laredo to Güemes:

The next stage leads you from Laredo to Güemes, covering approximately 29 km. You'll traverse coastal and rural landscapes, including the fascinating marshlands of Santoña and Noja.
Difficulty: Moderate/Challenging.

From Güemes to Santander:

After leaving Güemes, you'll reach Santander, covering about 12 km. This stage features a mix of coastal and urban scenery, with a few challenging ascents along the way.
Difficulty: Moderate.

From Santander to Santillana del Mar:

Continuing on to Santillana del Mar, you'll walk about 38 km through rural landscapes. This segment can be demanding, with several hilly sections to navigate.
Difficulty: Challenging.

From Santillana del Mar to Comillas:

The following stage takes you to Comillas, covering approximately 22 km through the Oyambre Natural Park. The route can be challenging in some parts.
Difficulty: Moderate/Challenging.

From Comillas to Colombres:

You'll reach Colombres after walking about 28.8 km through hilly and rural terrain, leaving the region of Cantabria and entering Asturias.
Difficulty: Moderate.

From Colombres to Llanes:

Continuing along the path, you'll arrive in Llanes after about 23 km, passing through coastal and urban areas. Llanes is a village rich in natural beauty and artistic heritage, including the palace of Count de la Vega del Sella.
Difficulty: Easy.

From Llanes to Ribadesella:

The next leg of your journey takes you from Llanes to Ribadesella, covering around 32 km. Ribadesella is well-known for its canoe descents on the Sella River and the famous Tito Bustillo cave.
Difficulty: Moderate/Challenging.

From Ribadesella to Sebrayo:

Continuing along the coast, you'll reach Sebrayo after walking approximately 22 km. This stage offers sweeping views of the coast and traverses rural areas.
Difficulty: Moderate.

From Sebrayo to Gijón:

After Sebrayo, you'll head towards Gijón, covering about 35.8 km through coastal and urban landscapes. From Sebrayo, you also have the option to detour to Oviedo and continue on the Original Way.
Difficulty: Challenging.

From Gijón to Avilés:

This stage leads you from Gijón to Avilés, covering approximately 25 km. Avilés is known for its historic center, recognized as an area of artistic and monumental significance, and its expansive beaches.
Difficulty: Moderate/Challenging.

From Avilés to Soto de Luiña:

As you continue, you'll arrive at Soto de Luiña after covering roughly 38.5 km. On the way, you'll pass through the town of Muros De Nalón, a popular halfway stop for many pilgrims (the distance between Avilés and Muros De Nalón is about 22.5 km).
Difficulty: Moderate/Challenging (depending on where you choose to stop).

From Soto de Luiña to Luarca:

The next stage takes you from Soto de Luiña to Luarca, covering about 33 km. About 18.5 km from Soto De Luiña, you can make an intermediate stop in the town of Cadavedo.

Difficulty: Moderate/Challenging (depending on where you choose to stop).

From Luarca to La Caridad:

Continuing along the coast, you'll reach La Caridad after walking approximately 29.5 km, crossing the Navia River as you approach the capital of the Franco council.

Difficulty: Easy.

From La Caridad to Ribadeo:

Following the route, you'll arrive in Ribadeo after covering about 29.5 km, where you can admire the beautiful Moreno Tower.

Difficulty: Easy.

From Ribadeo to Lourenzá:

The next leg of the journey takes you from Ribadeo to Lourenzá, covering about 28 km, where you'll have the chance to see the Tovar Castle.

Difficulty: Moderate/Challenging.

From Lourenzá to Abadín:

Continuing towards Abadín, you'll travel about 25 km through small villages, forests, and stunning landscapes. Some sections of this stage may be more challenging.

Difficulty: Moderate/Challenging.

From Abadín to Vilalba:

You'll reach Vilalba after walking approximately 27 km through a flat stage with expansive green grasslands.

Difficulty: Easy/Moderate.

From Vilalba to Baamonde:

The next stage, taking you from Vilalba to Baamonde over 18 km, features flat terrain where you'll cross the Magdalena and Trimaz rivers.
Difficulty: Easy.

From Baamonde to Miraz:

Continuing on, you'll reach Miraz after covering about 15 km, crossing a level railroad track and a medieval bridge along the way.
Difficulty: Easy.

From Miraz to Sobrado dos Monxes:

In this 25 km stage, you'll enjoy a sense of unmatched tranquility and a deep connection with nature as you traverse paths once walked by Galician Celtic tribes.
Difficulty: Moderate/Challenging.

From Sobrado dos Monxes to Arzúa:

Continuing towards Arzúa, you'll cover about 21.5 km through rural and hilly landscapes. This will be the "final" stage of the Northern Way, as the next stage will merge with the French Way (for more details, see page 29).
Difficulty: Moderate/Challenging.

Interest Places (Cathedrals, Museums) and Iconic Landmarks

Dear Pilgrim, as you embark on the enchanting journey of the Northern Way, you will find yourself surrounded by a wealth of landmarks, cathedrals, museums and iconic sites that enrich the pilgrimage experience. We'll touch on just a few highlights here (covering them all would turn this guide into a novel), leaving you to discover many more on your path.

From Irún to San Sebastián:

Your adventure begins in Irún, where the panoramic views of the Pyrenees will leave you in awe. Early on, you'll encounter the first treasure of your journey, the San Marcial  Cathedral. This Gothic cathedral, built between the 13th and 14th centuries, is dedicated to the city's patron saint. Its interior features polychrome stained glass and sacred art that narrate centuries of history. As you continue, you'll arrive in San Sebastián, where the picturesque Basilica of Santa Maria del Coro (image) greets you with its ornate Gothic façade. Take a moment to relax on La Concha Beach, enjoying the view of the Cantabrian Sea and the surrounding mountains.

From Zarautz to Deba:

On the stretch from Zarautz to Deba, you'll pass the Sanctuary of San Telmo, a sacred site dedicated to the patron saint of sailors. Legend has it that an icon of the saint was found floating in the sea, and the sense of spirituality is palpable as you walk these hilly paths.

From Markina-Xemein to Gernika-Lumo:
Between Markina-Xemein and Gernika-Lumo, you'll come across the Casa de Juntas, a symbol of Basque democracy. This historic building houses the famous Tree of Gernika, where Basque leaders are sworn in. Visiting this site offers a deep dive into the heart of Basque identity and its centuries-old history.

From Lezama to Bilbao:
As you continue to Bilbao, you'll be greeted by the magnificent Santiago Cathedral, a Gothic masterpiece dating back to the 14th century, adorned with numerous  chapels and the statue of Santiago Matamoros. Nearby, the Guggenheim Museum (image) offers a modern art experience, housed in an iconic building designed by Frank Gehry.

From Vilalba to Baamonde:
On the route from Vilalba to Baamonde, you'll encounter the Monastery of Santa María de Xunqueira de Espadañedo. Founded in the 13th century, this Romanesque complex features well-preserved medieval frescoes that transport you back in time.

From Soto de Luiña to Luarca:
As you travel from Soto de Luiña to Luarca, the Church of Santa Eulalia will catch your eye. This 12th-century Romanesque building is noted for its charming square-shaped bell tower and intricate architectural details.

From La Caridad to Ribadeo:
Continuing from La Caridad to Ribadeo, you'll arrive at
the Moreno Tower
(image), an old lighthouse
that once guided sailors
through the treacherous
coastal waters. The
panoramic views from the
tower are breathtaking,
offering a unique chance to reflect on the vastness of the
seascape.

Panoramic Views of the Galician Mountains:
As you approach Santiago de Compostela, you'll traverse
the Galician Mountains, a mountain range that adds a
spectacular finale to your journey. The sweeping views and
the sense of achievement from conquering these heights are
integral to the culmination of your pilgrimage.

From O Pedrouzo to Santiago de Compostela:
Finally, your remarkable pilgrimage will reach its peak in
Santiago de Compostela,
where the grand Cathedral
awaits. Pilgrims gather in
Obradoiro Square to
admire its façade, and the
interior is even more
magnificent, featuring the
Sanctuary of the Holy
Sepulcher and the reliquary
of the apostle James. The "Botafumeiro", a giant censer,
adds a mystical touch to the solemn masses.

THE ENGLISH WAY

Characteristics, Practical Advice and Stages

Dear Pilgrim, if you've chosen to embark on this journey, which spans approximately 112 km, you owe a debt of gratitude to the people of the  Scandinavian countries (like Norway, Sweden, Denmark, Finland and Iceland) and especially to the English, Scots and Irish. It was they who played a key role in shaping what we now know as the "English Way". Arriving in Galicia by sea from their respective ports, they reached Ferrol or La Coruña, where strategically located ports helped establish and increase the popularity of this route.

Now, let's explore the key aspects to consider when taking on this path.

Physical and Mental Preparation:

Prepare yourself physically for the journey, even though the English Way is often considered less strenuous than other routes. It's still important to be in good shape, incorporating long walks or hikes into your routine to get accustomed to covering long distances and helping your body adapt to the ongoing physical demands.

Timing and Weather:

The ideal times to walk this route are in the spring (from March to May) and, although it might be rainy, in autumn (from September to October, and sometimes November, depending on the year). These periods offer milder temperatures and fewer tourists. In contrast, winter brings very low temperatures and the possibility of some accommodations being closed due to the "low season", while summer, though doable, can bring extremely high temperatures in less shaded areas.

Accommodation and Lodging:
Carefully plan where you'll stay along the way. The options vary, including hostels, inns, B&Bs and "albergues". It's a good idea to book your accommodations in advance, especially during busy periods, to ensure you have a place to rest each night.

Navigation and Signage:
On the English Way, the signage is well-organized and easy to follow. You'll find yellow arrows along the route that guide you in the right direction. These signs are strategically placed, making it easy to navigate the journey even without a detailed map.

Starting Points, Stages and Distances:

The English Way can commence from either Ferrol or La Coruña. If you're considering <u>starting from Ferrol</u>, **READ ON**:

From Ferrol to Neda:

Beginning your journey in Ferrol, the first stage to Neda covers approximately 20 km. You'll traverse a mix of coastal and urban landscapes, with a mostly flat terrain making for an easy and smooth start.
<u>Difficulty: Easy</u>.

From Neda to Pontedeume:

Continuing from Neda to Pontedeume, a distance of around 20 km, the path follows the coastline, leading you through Neda and on to the medieval town of Pontedeume, known for its fortress. The varied terrain remains accessible to walkers of all experience levels.
Difficulty: Easy.

From Pontedeume to Betanzos:

Traveling about 20 km from Pontedeume to Betanzos, you'll explore coastal scenery and pass through wooded areas as you approach Betanzos, a town famous for its medieval churches. This stage introduces a moderate level of difficulty, adding a bit more challenge.
Difficulty: Moderate.

From Betanzos to Bruma:

Covering roughly 18 km, the route from Betanzos to Bruma takes you through forested areas and rural paths, leading to Bruma where the Church of San Xiao is a cultural highlight. The terrain is varied but manageable.
Difficulty: Moderate.

• If you choose to start in La Coruña, your journey will begin with the following stage; so, start **READING FROM HERE**. If you started from Ferrol, however, you'll skip this next stage.

From La Coruña to Bruma:

Starting in La Coruña, head towards Bruma, covering approximately 28 km across a mix of coastal and rural terrains.
Difficulty: Moderate.

• At this point, the two "variants" merge, so the stages will be the same no matter where you began.

From Bruma to Sigueiro:

This 24 km stage from Bruma to Sigueiro continues through rural landscapes and small villages. Although some sections are longer, they are not particularly challenging.
Difficulty: Moderate.

From Sigueiro to Santiago de Compostela:

The final stretch, about 15 km, takes you to Santiago de Compostela, passing through woods and suburban areas. The shorter distance makes this last stage accessible to all.
Difficulty: Easy.

Interest Places (Cathedrals, Museums) and Iconic Landmarks

Dear pilgrim, on this journey, you will encounter numerous curiosities, attractions and unique places. Listing them all would make it impossible to keep this guide in a "pocket-sized" format. However, as with the other routes, I'd like to highlight a few spots that I strongly recommend you visit.

From Ferrol to Neda:
Your journey begins in Ferrol, and in the first 20 km stretch to Neda, take a moment to admire the Tower of Andrade, a medieval structure that stands as a testament to the region's rich history.

From Neda to Pontedeume:
Continuing from Neda, the route follows the coast and leads you to Pontedeume, a medieval town known for its fortress. In Pontedeume's historic center, be sure to stop and explore the Convento de las Virtudes, a 14th-century Franciscan monastery steeped in history.

From Pontedeume to Betanzos:
Traveling roughly 20 km from Pontedeume to Betanzos, you'll reach the historic center, where you can visit the Iglesia de San Francisco, a Gothic treasure with a captivating cloister.

From La Coruña to Bruma:
If your journey starts in La Coruña, consider visiting the Torre de Hércules (image) before reaching Bruma. This ancient Roman lighthouse, a UNESCO World Heritage  site, is a remarkable symbol of the city's maritime heritage.

From Betanzos to Bruma:
Continuing from Betanzos to Bruma, the Church of San Xiao is a cultural highlight worth visiting. Along the way, you might also come across the Cruz de los Franceses, a cross that tells the legend of the locals' hospitality towards pilgrims.

From Bruma to Sigueiro:

As your journey continues towards Sigueiro, take the time to visit the "Paseo de Los Olivos" (Promenade of the Olive Trees) at Pazo de Santa Cruz de Rivadulla, known for its impressive beauty and uniqueness.

From Sigueiro to Santiago de Compostela:

In the final stage of this route, you'll reach Santiago de Compostela. The sight of the spires of the Cathedral of Santiago de Compostela will be the grand culmination of your journey, offering you a chance to immerse yourself in the city's rich history.

THE PORTUGUESE WAY

Characteristics, Practical Advice and Stages

Dear pilgrim, if you've chosen the Portuguese Way, which spans approximately 640 km, your journey begins in Lisbon, where you'll be immersed in the vibrant energy of the Portuguese capital. Before setting out on your walk, take the time to explore the city, indulging in its delicious local cuisine and admiring its historical landmarks. Don't miss a visit to Lisbon Cathedral, a site rich in history and spirituality.

One distinctive feature of the Portuguese Way is the choice between the inland route and the coastal variant. If you're drawn to stunning views of the Atlantic Ocean and a cooler experience, you might prefer the coastal path. However, keep in mind that while this route offers breathtaking marine vistas and the refreshing ocean breeze, it can also be more challenging than the inland option.

Timing and Weather:

From a climatic perspective, the best times to embark on the Portuguese Way are during spring and autumn, when temperatures are milder and the weather is generally more conducive to an enjoyable walk. It's advisable to avoid the summer months, as the heat can become quite intense, making the journey more strenuous.

Navigation and Signage:

The signage along the Portuguese Way is well-organized and easy to follow; simply look for the yellow arrows and shell symbols that will guide you smoothly along the path. It's a good idea to keep a map (either digital or paper) with you to ensure you stay on course.

Starting Points, Stages and Distances:

Lisbona ➜ Verdelha de Baixo:

Begin your pilgrimage in Lisbon, the captivating capital of Portugal, known for its remarkable neighborhoods. Explore the elegant Baixa district and the unique charm of Alfama. Your first stop is Verdelha de Baixo, a distance of about 22.3 km.
Difficulty: Easy.

Verdelha de Baixo ➜ Azambuja:

Continue on the next leg, covering 20 km from Verdelha de Baixo to Azambuja. Along this stretch, you'll be accompanied by the constant presence of the tracks and the nearby highway.
Difficulty: Easy.

Azambuja ➜ Santarém:

Your journey then takes you from Azambuja to Santarém, a distance of 32.6 km. Here, you'll have the opportunity to admire the "Gothic capital" of Portugal, with its stunning cathedral and the Church of Nossa Senhora da Conceição as prime examples.
Difficulty: Moderate.

Santarém ➜ Golegã:

Covering 32.5 km, the path leads from Santarém to Golegã. This city is renowned as the birthplace of the writer,

playwright and journalist José Saramago, and for hosting the National Horse Fair.
Difficulty: Moderate.

Golegã ➜ Tomar:

Covering 30.4 km, the route from Golegã to Tomar takes you to a city that once served as the headquarters of the Templar Order, where you can marvel at its impressive castle. Tomar is also renowned for the Tabuleiros festival, one of the oldest and most celebrated in Portugal.
Difficulty: Moderate.

Tomar ➜ Alvaiázere:

The journey from Tomar to Alvaiázere spans 31.7 km. Along the way, you'll cross several bridges, including Peniche, which was part of an ancient communication route between Tomar and Coimbra.
Difficulty: Moderate.

Alvaiázere ➜ Rabaçal:

Travel 31.6 km from Alvaiázere to Rabaçal, where you will encounter the remnants of the majestic Germanelo Castle.
Difficulty: Moderate.

Rabaçal ➜ Coimbra:

Spanning 28.9 km, the route continues from Rabaçal to Coimbra, a city full of beautiful churches, villas, and parks that bring vibrancy to this historic location.
Difficulty: Moderate.

Coimbra ➜ Sernadelo:

Walk 25.1 km from Coimbra to Sernadelo, a stage where the landscape is dominated by urban settings with fewer natural elements.
Difficulty: Moderate.

Sernadelo ➜ Águeda:

The next leg covers 24.9 km from Sernadelo to Águeda, a city nestled by the Águeda River and famous for hosting the largest natural lake on the Iberian Peninsula, "A Pateira de Fermentelos".
Difficulty: Easy.

Águeda ➜ Albergaria-a-Nova:

Travel 21.6 km from Águeda to Albergaria-a-Nova. This stage serves as a transitional segment, offering an easy walk that is accessible to most pilgrims.
Difficulty: Easy.

Albergaria-a-Nova ➜ São João da Madeira:

This stage takes you along a relatively straightforward path, covering about 22.2 km from Albergaria-a-Nova to São João da Madeira. You'll follow the old medieval road, crossing through charming streets.
Difficulty: Moderate.

São João da Madeira ➜ Grijó:

Journey 19.6 km from São João da Madeira to Grijó, encountering varied terrains and occasional ascents that add a bit of excitement to your pilgrimage. This stage is manageable for most walkers.
Difficulty: Moderate.

Grijó ➜ Porto:

Conclude this portion of your journey with a 15.6 km walk from Grijó to Porto. The path is relatively easy, featuring flat terrain with no major challenges. Enjoy the final stretch into Porto, a UNESCO World Heritage city, with scenic views and a comfortable walk.
Difficulty: Easy.

Porto ➜ Vairão:

Start the next phase with a 25.4 km journey from Porto, Portugal's second-largest city, to Vairão. Take the opportunity to explore Porto's narrow streets before continuing on a route that mixes terrains with some moderate ascents, leading you to Vairão.
Difficulty: Moderate.

Vairão ➜ São Pedro de Rates:

Walk 13.3 km from Vairão to São Pedro de Rates along a relatively easy path with flat terrain, ideal for a more relaxed pilgrimage. Enjoy the picturesque landscapes and a gentle walk.
Difficulty: Easy.

São Pedro de Rates ➜ Barcelos:

Continue your journey with a 16.1 km walk from São Pedro de Rates to Barcelos, a city famous for the legend of the "Gallo de Barcelos", a symbol of Portuguese identity.
Difficulty: Moderate.

Barcelos ➜ Ponte de Lima:

Cover 34.3 km from Barcelos to Ponte de Lima in a

more demanding stage due to its length. Along the way, you'll pass several churches and a medieval bridge.
Difficulty: Challenging.

Ponte de Lima ➜ Rubiães:

Today, you'll walk 17.6 km along the banks of the Labruja River, surrounded by stunning mountains and forests, with only a slight challenge during the ascent to the summit of Portela Grande.
Difficulty: Moderate.

Rubiães ➜ Tui:

On this stage, you'll cover around 19 km as you continue to approach the long-awaited goal of reaching the Apostle James.
Difficulty: Moderate.

Tui ➜ Redondela:

Cross into Spain and journey 32.5 km from Tui to Redondela. Along this section, you'll encounter a passage between the public hostel of Mos and the chapel of Santiaguiño, with a 145-meter elevation gain. As a reward for your effort, you'll be surrounded by beautiful landscapes at the end of the stage.
Difficulty: Moderate.

*Redondela ➜ Pontevedra:

This is a shorter stage of about 19 km, with minimal inclines. I recommend concluding the stage upon reaching Pontevedra, as this city boasts a rich historical heritage, second only to Santiago de Compostela in Galicia.
Difficulty: Easy.

Pontevedra ➜ Caldas de Reis:

In this 19 km stage, you'll pass through several towns and villages that are characteristic of the Galician countryside. The route crosses the national road at various points, weaving between small villages that will accompany you throughout the journey.

Difficulty: Moderate.

Caldas de Reis ➜ Padrón:

Cover 18.5 km from Caldas de Reis to Padrón. This stage offers a moderate challenge with varied terrain and occasional ascents, making for an exciting approach to your final destination.

Difficulty: Moderate.

*Padrón ➜ Santiago de Compostela:

In this final stretch of 25 km, you'll pass through numerous villages and neighborhoods, just as the disciples of Santiago did when they brought his remains to what would become his eternal resting place.

Difficulty: Moderate.

THE COASTAL OR LITORAL VARIANT

The coastal variant diverges from the central route in the city of Porto, where the pilgrimage takes a different path that, as the name suggests, allows you to walk along the coast of Portugal. Here are the stages that differ from the Central Route, eventually merging back in the city of Redondela:

Porto ➔ Labruge:

Start your coastal journey in Porto, covering 24.5 km to reach Labruge. This stage is relatively easy as it follows the coastline along flat terrain, crossing multiple beaches with wooden walkways and a bike path that offers stunning views of the Atlantic Ocean.
Difficulty: Easy.

Labruge ➔ Póvoa de Varzim:

Travel 14 km from Labruge to Póvoa de Varzim, a city renowned for its beaches and culinary delights. Along the way, you'll pass sites such as the Castro de Sampaio, the ruins of an ancient Iron Age village; the Mindelo Ornithological Reserve; and the 16th-century Santa Maria Church in Azurara, near the Ave River. This stage is rich in cultural experiences, so plan according to your interests and available time.
Difficulty: Easy.

Póvoa de Varzim ➔ Marinhas:

Cover 24.5 km from Póvoa de Varzim to Marinhas. This stage features a mix of landscapes, some along the coast with beautiful beaches and others on simpler road stretches.
Difficulty: Moderate.

Marinhas ➔ Viana do Castelo:

In this 20.8 km stage, you'll leave the beaches and coastal views behind, but you'll still have the chance to explore the historic center of the quaint town of Viana do Castelo.
Difficulty: Moderate.

Viana do Castelo ➜ Caminha:

Walk 26.8 km from Viana do Castelo to Caminha. During this phase, you'll reach the border of Portugal with Spain in Galicia, enjoying the final kilometers with expansive, glistening views of the Atlantic Ocean.
Difficulty: Moderate.

Caminha ➜ Puerto de Mougás:

Finally, you'll arrive in Galicia after crossing the Minho River by ferry, leaving Caminha and Portuguese lands behind, having covered approximately 23.5 km.
Difficulty: Moderate.

Puerto de Mougás ➜ San Pedro de la Ramallosa:

Travel 16 km from Puerto de Mougás to San Pedro de la Ramallosa. You might also choose to end this stage in Baiona, where a villa offers a splendid view. In that case, the distance would be about 14 km, adding a couple of kilometers to the next day's journey.
Difficulty: Easy.

San Pedro de la Ramallosa ➜ Vigo:

In this penultimate stage, you'll decide whether to continue to Vigo via the Official Camino, marked by yellow arrows, or take the route closer to the ocean, marked by green arrows. The distance for this stage is approximately 22.5 km.
Difficulty: Moderate.

Vigo ➜ Redondela:

This 16 km stage offers one of the best views toward the

Ría de Vigo as you walk along the Senda da Traída das Augas. Additionally, this stage will reconnect you with the Central Portuguese Way (see asterisk (*) on p.55).
Difficulty: Easy.

THE SPIRITUAL VARIANT

The Spiritual Variant of Pontevedra is a captivating route within the Portuguese Way, spanning 73 kilometers across four stages. This variant can be easily incorporated into the Portuguese Way, requiring no more than five days to complete. According to the legend of the "Traslatio", "Finis Terrae (Finisterre)" was the furthest point reached by St. James, and his remains were transported by boat to Galicia. This variant replicates that journey, including a crossing of the Ulla River.

Pontevedra ➜ Combarro:

Begin your spiritual journey in Pontevedra, following the stunning coastline for approximately 20 km to reach Combarro. This stage takes you through the picturesque villages of Poio and Campelo, offering breathtaking views of the Ría de Pontevedra.
Difficulty: Easy/Moderate.

Combarro ➜ Vilanova de Arousa:

Continue your pilgrimage, covering around 17 km from Combarro to Vilanova de Arousa. This stage features a beautiful coastal walk, passing through "A Seara" and providing peaceful moments by the sea.
Difficulty: Moderate.

Vilanova de Arousa ➜ Pontecesures (Traslatio):

Experience the historic "Traslatio" in this 25-kilometer stage from Vilanova de Arousa to Pontecesures. The route follows the course of the Ulla River, passing through Bamio, Catoira and Vilarello. Admire the impressive Torres de Catoira, which hold significance in Viking history.

Difficulty: Moderate/Challenging.

Pontecesures ➜ Padrón:

Conclude your spiritual journey with a 9-kilometer walk from Pontecesures to Padrón. This final stage allows you to visit the renowned Padrón in the Church of Santiago, a symbolic site linked to the arrival of the Apostle James's boat, connecting you with the last stage of the Central Portuguese Way (see asterisk (*) on p.56).

Difficulty: Easy.

Interest Places (Cathedrals, Museums) and Iconic Landmarks

Lisbon:

Begin your journey in the magnificent city of Lisbon, known as the city of seven hills. Wander through the Alfama district, where you'll find the  Lisbon Cathedral, a stunning example of Romanesque architecture that has withstood the test of time, including numero us earthquakes and invasions. Be sure to cross the "25 de Abril" Bridge (image), which offers a breathtaking view of the city and the Tagus River, especially at sunset, creating an unforgettable experience.

Coimbra:

Coimbra, often referred to as the "City of Students", is a place rich in academic history. Explore the historic University of Coimbra, established in 1290, and marvel at the Joanina Library, a Baroque masterpiece housing a collection of rare manuscripts. The university's courtyards and amphitheaters echo with centuries of scholarly pursuit and cultural heritage.

Porto:

Upon reaching Porto, immerse yourself in its distinctive charm. Discover the historic  Ribeira district (image), a UNESCO World Heritage Site. Porto Cathedral, showcasing Romanesque and Gothic elements, stands as a symbol of the city. For a different viewpoint, walk across the Dom Luís I Bridge and take in the stunning panorama of the Douro River. Don't miss the

Clérigos Tower, an iconic bell tower located in the heart of Porto.

Barcelos:

Barcelos is renowned for the legend of the "Rooster of Barcelos", a beloved symbol of Portuguese folklore. Visit the historic center and explore the Church of Bom Jesus da Cruz, where the famous legend originated.

Ponte de Lima:

In this picturesque town, take time to explore the Roman Bridge, a lasting emblem of Roman engineering, and enjoy a stroll along the scenic banks of the Lima River. The Matriz Church, with its Gothic façade and Baroque embellishments, stands as a testament to the enduring art and architecture of the ages.

Santiago de Compostela:

Your journey reaches its pinnacle in Santiago de Compostela, Spain. The Santiago Cathedral, with its grand façade and the relics of Saint James, serve s as the spiritual and symbolic heart of the Camino. If possible, attend the Pilgrim's Mass, a moment that will leave an

indelible mark on your pilgrimage experience.

THE ORIGINAL WAY

Characteristics, Practical Advice and Stages

Fellow pilgrim, it's important to know that the Original Way, also known as "The Way of the Kings" is a pilgrimage route  rich in history and spirituality. Its origins date back to the 9th century when the Asturian king Alfonso II embarked on a journey to visit the tomb of the apostle Saint James. Inspired by a dream in which Saint James revealed the location of his burial, the king followed a path that today forms the heart of the Original Way, stretching over 325 km.

Walking the "Camino Primitivo" means retracing the steps of those who, centuries ago, made this journey driven by faith and determination. Along the route, you'll come across ancient monasteries, Romanesque churches and roads that still preserve the essence of the medieval era.

Timing and Weather:

The Original Way can be traveled year-round, but the best time to embark on this journey is from May to September. During this period, rainfall is minimal, and temperatures are generally mild. The northern location of the route, along with the influence of the Atlantic, brings cool to moderate summer temperatures, typically not exceeding 25°C. However, it's wise to be prepared for rain, especially in the western regions. In the winter months, the climate becomes colder, with temperatures often dipping below freezing.

Physical Preparation:

The Original Way is known for its physical demands. The route includes challenging stages and significant elevation changes, requiring proper physical preparation. Training should focus on building cardiovascular endurance and leg strength. Activities such as long-distance walking, uphill and downhill hikes, and strength training will help prepare your body for the rigorous demands of the pilgrimage.

Navigation and Environment:

Signage along the Original Way is similar to other Camino routes, marked by yellow arrows and scallop shells to guide you. Be sure to respect the environment by adhering to "Leave No Trace" principles, helping to preserve the trail for future pilgrims.

Starting Points, Stages and Distances:

Oviedo ➜ Grado:

Set off on a 25 km journey from Oviedo to Grado. This stage introduces you to the historic city of Oviedo, where the San Salvador Cathedral sets the spiritual tone for your pilgrimage. The terrain is mostly flat, allowing you to ease into the Camino experience.
Difficulty: Moderate.

Grado ➜ Salas:

This 22 km stage from Grado to Salas takes you through a varied landscape of rural areas and woodlands. Salas welcomes you with its historic charm, adding a rich cultural aspect to your journey.
Difficulty: Moderate.

Salas ➜ Tineo:

Spanning 20 km, this stage offers moderate climbs and breathtaking panoramic views. Tineo, with its historic center, provides both cultural enrichment and spiritual respite for pilgrims.
Difficulty: Moderate.

Tineo ➜ Borres:

Cover a manageable 13 km route, offering scenic views of various landscapes that provide a preview of the challenges to come.
Difficulty: Easy.

1) **Borres ➜ Berducedo lungo la Ruta de los Hospitales**:

This 24 km stretch along the Ruta de los Hospitales is known for its breathtaking beauty. Although moderately challenging, the stunning views make the effort worthwhile.
Difficulty: Moderate.

2) **Borres ➜ Berducedo per Pola de Allande**:

Alternatively, take the 28.5 km route through Pola de Allande, one of the most picturesque stages with its cobbled streets and characteristic stone buildings. Though physically demanding, the beauty of the surroundings offers a rewarding experience.
Difficulty: Challenging.

Berducedo ➜ Grandas de Salime:

Travel 20.5 km on a relatively easy path, leading to Grandas de Salime, known for its impressive dam and

ethnographic museum, making this a culturally enriching stop.
Difficulty: Easy.

Grandas de Salime ➜ A Fonsagrada:

This 25 km route takes you through diverse landscapes and some ascents, eventually reaching the peaceful city of A Fonsagrada, perfect for rest and reflection.
Difficulty: Moderate.

A Fonsagrada ➜ O Cádavo:

Over 24.5 km, you'll encounter a variety of landscapes at a moderate difficulty level. Arriving in O Cádavo, you'll find the town's main restaurant, Elixio, near the church, offering a welcome spot for relaxation.
Difficulty: Moderate.

O Cádavo ➜ Lugo:

This 29.5 km stage is challenging due to its length. However, reaching Lugo, with its ancient Roman walls, rewards you with a rich cultural experience.
Difficulty: Challenging.

Lugo ➜ Ferreira:

Spanning 26.5 km, this stage presents moderate challenges but leads to the tranquil setting of Ferreira, offering a peaceful place to rest.
Difficulty: Moderate.

Ferreira ➜ Melide:

A relatively easy 20 km route takes you through relaxing

landscapes. Melide is famous for its gastronomy, inviting pilgrims to indulge in local delicacies.

Difficulty: Easy.

Melide ➜ O Pedrouzo:

This 33 km stage is demanding and requires careful physical preparation. O Pedrouzo serves as a strategic stop before the final leg of your journey.

Difficulty: Challenging.

O Pedrouzo ➜ Santiago de Compostela:

Conclude your pilgrimage with a 20 km stage to Santiago de Compostela, the final destination of the Original Way. This moderately challenging final stretch will leave you with unforgettable memories of the incredible adventure you've completed.

Difficulty: Moderate.

Interest Places (Cathedrals, Museums) and Iconic Landmarks

Your journey along the Original Way is rich with cultural and historical discoveries, made even more rewarding by the landmarks you'll encounter. Below are some examples of what you'll find along the route, offering the chance to explore and add depth to your pilgrimage:

Oviedo:
Begin your exploration in Oviedo, where the imposing Cathedral of San Salvador marks the spiritual start of your journey. This architectural marvel, dating back to the 9th century, is home to a golden altar that has captivated visitors for centuries. Wander through its grand naves and soak in the mystical atmosphere that envelops this sacred space.

Grado:
As you make your way to Grado, you'll come across more historical treasures. Founded in the 9th century, the city is home to the Mariluz Museum, a hidden gem that houses a collection of artifacts narrating the local history. Take time to appreciate medieval objects and artworks, offering a glimpse into the lives and stories of those who walked this path long ago.

Ruta de los Hospitales:
Continuing towards the Ruta de los Hospitales, you'll embark on a 24 km stage known for its stunning natural beauty. Along this route, the Monastery of Santa María Obona serves as a spiritual retreat. Established in the 10th century, this monastery stands as a testament to endurance and provides a peaceful sanctuary for reflection.

Grandas de Salime:

Arriving in Grandas de Salime, you'll be greeted by the impressive Salime Dam (image), creating a large artificial lake. Built in the 1950s for hydroelectric power, this landmark offers a unique  glimpse into the technological advancements that have shaped the Camino's history.

Lugo:

In Lugo, the majestic Roman Walls (image), designated as a UNESCO World Heritage Site, will undoubtedly capture your attention. Constructed in the 3rd century, these walls are a striking reminder of the Roman Empire's  grandeur. Walk along the walls' pathway and let yourself be transported back in time.

Santiago de Compostela:

At the culmination of your pilgrimage, Santiago de Compostela's Cathedral welcomes you with its intricate façade and towering spires. Inside, you'll find the Portico de la Gloria, a masterpiece from the 12th century that has been beautifully restored. This extraordinary work of Romanesque art serves as a  powerful symbol of your journey's completion. Be sure to touch the revered statue of Saint James, marking the conclusion of your pilgrimage and immersing yourself in the ancient heritage of the Original Way.

THE SILVER WAY

Characteristics, Practical Advice and Stages

Dear pilgrim, if you've chosen to embark on the Silver Way (or "Via de la Plata"), prepare for an extraordinary journey that spans Spain from south to north, offering breathtaking landscapes and rich cultural experiences. As one of the longest Camino routes, stretching nearly 1,000  kilometers, it's essential to carefully plan your daily stages based on your physical abilities and travel preferences. Take the time to study the map and create a realistic itinerary that suits your pace.

A key highlight of this route is its deep historical significance, so make sure to explore the historical landmarks along the way, including ancient Roman temples and captivating medieval cities.

Time and Weather:

The climate on the Silver Way varies greatly, with hot summers and cooler winters. Be sure to pack light clothing for sunny days and thermal layers for the cooler evenings. A reliable rain jacket is a must, as rainfall can be unpredictable.

Navigation and Signage:

Like other St. James routes, the Silver Way is marked with yellow arrows and the scallop shell, clearly guiding your path.

Local Cuisine:

The food along the Silver Way is rich in flavor and deeply rooted in regional traditions. Enjoy the variety of Spanish tapas and be sure to try local specialties along your journey.

Physical and Mental Preparation:

The Silver Way requires a good level of physical fitness. Before setting out, ensure you've trained well, focusing on cardiovascular endurance and leg strength. During the walk, it's important to take regular breaks to rest your feet and care for your body.

Starting Points, Stages and Distances:

Sevilla ➜ Guillena:

Begin your journey with a stage of about 23 km from Seville, the capital of Andalusia. This initial transition takes you from the city into the rural landscape, crossing mostly flat terrain before reaching Guillena.
Difficulty: Easy.

Guillena ➜ Castilblanco de los Arroyos:

Travel about 18 km from Guillena to Castilblanco de los Arroyos. This stage takes you through gentle hills and agricultural landscapes, offering an early glimpse of the natural beauty that defines the Silver Way.
Difficulty: Moderate.

Castilblanco de los Arroyos ➜ Almadén de la Plata:

Cover around 29 km from Castilblanco de los Arroyos, passing through Los Berrocales Park and across vast meadows and rolling hills dotted with farms, eventually leading to Almadén de la Plata.
Difficulty: Moderate.

Almadén de la Plata ➜ Monesterio:

Continue for about 34 km from Almadén de la Plata to Monesterio. This stretch takes you through rural landscapes, forests, vast fields and several streams, giving you a taste of the serene Spanish countryside.
Difficulty: Moderate.

Monesterio ➜ Fuente de Cantos:

Cover around 21 km from Monesterio to Fuente de Cantos, the birthplace of renowned painter Francisco de Zurbarán.
Difficulty: Easy.

Fuente de Cantos ➜ Zafra:

Travel roughly 24.6 km from Fuente de Cantos to Zafra, crossing primarily flat terrain. Zafra offers a fascinating historical heritage to explore.
Difficulty: Easy.

Zafra ➜ Villafranca De Los Barros:

Walk about 19 km from Zafra to Villafranca De Los Barros. This shorter stage provides time to visit the beautiful Gothic-Renaissance church and stroll through the "city of music".
Difficulty: Easy.

Villafranca De Los Barros ➜ Torremejía:

Advance approximately 27 km to Torremejía, famously featured in Camilo José Cela's novel "La familia de Pascual Duarte".
Difficulty: Easy.

Torremejía ➜ Mérida:

Travel around 16 km to Mérida, a city founded by Emperor Octavian Augustus and once the capital of the Visigothic Kingdom of Spain, located by the Guadiana River.
Difficulty: Easy.

Mérida ➜ Alcuescar:

Cover approximately 36.5 km, passing through Cornalvo Natural Park and the Proserpina Roman dam, a UNESCO World Heritage Site, before reaching Alcuescar.
Difficulty: Moderate/Challenging.

Alcuescar ➜ Cáceres:

Walk 38.2 km from Alcuescar to Cáceres. This longer stage introduces you to Cáceres, a city known for its medieval architecture.
Difficulty: Challenging.

Cáceres ➜ Embalse de Alcántara:

Tackle around 33.4 km from Cáceres to Embalse de Alcántara, crossing rural landscapes and reaching the stunning Alcántara Reservoir.
Difficulty: Challenging.

Embalse de Alcántara ➜ Grimaldo:

Cover about 21 km from Embalse de Alcántara, passing "Alto de los Castaños" at around 500 meters above sea level before descending towards Grimaldo.
Difficulty: Moderate.

Grimaldo ➜ Carcaboso:

Walk approximately 31 km from Grimaldo to Carcaboso, through peaceful fields and mountains, passing Galisteo's fortified walls and the tower of "La Picota".
Difficulty: Moderate.

Carcaboso ➜ Aldeanueva del Camino:

Travel 38.6 km from Carcaboso to Aldeanueva del Camino, with a highlight being the famous Roman arch of Cáparra, an impressive monument preserved over time.
Difficulty: Challenging.

Aldeanueva del Camino ➜ La Calzada de Béjar:

Today, you'll cross from the Extremadura region into Castile and León via the Béjar pass, covering a distance of about 22 km.
Difficulty: Moderate.

La Calzada de Béjar ➜ Fuenterroble de Salvatierra:

After several long stages, this 20 km stretch offers a chance to rest and savor the local Salamanca specialties, such as the renowned Guijuelo ham.
Difficulty: Easy.

Fuenterroble de Salvatierra ➜ San Pedro de Rozados:

This stage involves an ascent towards Pico de la Dueña, nearly 1,200 meters above sea level. Although the climb isn't steep, the starting elevation is over 900 meters. After the ascent, you'll descend to the Mendigos stream, with an optional detour through Pedrosillo de los Aires and Monterrubio de la Sierra, covering a total of 28.6 km.
Difficulty: Moderate.

San Pedro de Rozados ➜ Salamanca:

This stage takes you through natural areas, mostly forests and meadows, with Salamanca gradually appearing on the horizon. At 23 km, this stage offers the perfect opportunity to explore Salamanca's historic sites, such as Plaza Mayor, the Old and New Cathedrals, the Convent of San Esteban, the Casa de las Conchas and La Clerecía.
Difficulty: Easy.

Salamanca ➜ El Cubo de Tierra del Vino:

Be sure to stock up on supplies before starting this 36.4 km stage, as services are sparse along the route. The path runs parallel to the N-630, along a gravel road.
Difficulty: Challenging.

El Cubo de Tierra del Vino ➜ Zamora:

Continue for around 31.8 km from El Cubo de Tierra del Vino to Zamora, where the historic center, declared a Historical-Artistic Complex, showcases many Romanesque buildings, including the impressive cathedral.
Difficulty: Moderate/Challenging.

Zamora ➜ Montamarta:

Travel about 18.5 km from Zamora to Montamarta, an area known as the "land of bread" due to its abundant cereal fields. Be sure to sample local sweets like aceitadas, rebojos, mantecadas, orejas and bollos, all made with wheat flour.
Difficulty: Easy.

Montamarta ➜ Granja de Moreruela:

Walk around 23 km from Montamarta to Granja de

Moreruela, a stage characterized by constant climbs and descents through dirt paths. The journey is rewarded by sights such as Castrotorafe Castle and the Moreruela Monastery.
Difficulty: Easy.

Granja de Moreruela ➜ Benavente:

Cover about 27 km from Granja de Moreruela to Benavente, passing abandoned railway tracks that add a special, adventurous charm to this stretch.
Difficulty: Easy.

Benavente ➜ Alija del Infantado:

This shorter stage of about 22 km follows the Jamuz River, passing through towns like Villabrázaro, Maire de Castroponce and Puente de la Vizana. Although services are limited, the short distance makes this less of an issue.
Difficulty: Easy.

Alija del Infantado ➜ La Bañeza:

Walk around 22 km from Alija del Infantado to La Bañeza, replacing cereal fields with olive groves and vineyards, eventually reaching fields of poppies and wheat.
Difficulty: Easy.

La Bañeza ➜ Astorga:

Cover about 24.5 km from La Bañeza to Astorga. Once in the city, take time to visit the Episcopal Palace, the Cathedral of Santa Maria, the Medieval Wall, the Church of San Francisco and the Roman Gate. At this point, the Silver Way merges with the French Way, so refer to page 27 of this guide for the next stage marked with an asterisk (*).
Difficulty: Moderate.

Interest Places (Cathedrals, Museums) and Iconic Landmarks

Dear traveler, as you make your way along the Silver Way, you'll be immersed in an extraordinary journey through centuries of history, with monuments, cathedrals and museums enriching your experience on this ancient route. Here are just a few highlights you won't want to miss!

Almadén de la Plata:

In the charming town of Almadén de la Plata, the Collegiate Church of Santa Maria dell'Assunzione stands out with its striking Gothic architecture. Constructed in the 15th century, this church has been a testament to centuries of devotion and culture. Inside, you'll find frescoes and sculptures that bring biblical stories to life, while the main altar showcases exquisite inlay work.

Zafra:

Zafra is home to the magnificent Dukes of Feria Palace (image), a Renaissance masterpiece built in the 15th century. This palace is an example of architectural splendor, with interiors featuring rooms adorned with detailed stucco work and frescoes that illustrate the  lives of ancient nobility. The peaceful courtyard provides a glimpse into the elegance of court life from long ago.

Villafranca De Los Barros:

At the heart of Villafranca De Los Barros lies the Church of Santa María, a Gothic-Renaissance marvel. Its grand naves lead to ornately decorated altars and side chapels, housing sacred works of art. This church has been a witness to significant historical events, and as you walk through its columns, you can almost hear the echoes of prayers from centuries past.

Cáceres:

Cáceres greets you with its historic old town, a UNESCO World Heritage site. As you wander through its cobbled streets, be sure to visit the Concathedral of Santa María, which blends Romanesque and Gothic architectural styles.

Zamora:

Step back in time in the medieval city of Zamora by visiting its Cathedral, a remarkable example of Romanesque architecture. Inside, the Baroque altar and side chapels tell stories of faith and artistry. You can also explore the Diocesan Museum, where sacred art, liturgical objects and ancient manuscripts offer insights into the religious and cultural history of the region.

Salamanca:

In Salamanca, you'll be greeted by the splendor of Plaza Mayor. Take a seat at a café and admire the Baroque architecture surrounding the square. The Old and New Cathedrals (image) combine vario us architectural styles, with interiors that impress with their intricate details. Don't miss the Casa de las  Conchas, famous for its shell-adorned façade, where you can explore its history and collection of ancient texts.

CHAPTER 4: SAFETY & HELPFUL TIPS

SUPPORT & ASSISTANCE ALONG THE WAY

How to Find Help When Needed

Embarking on the Camino de Santiago is an enriching and memorable experience, but it's natural to feel some concerns regarding safety and assistance throughout your journey. Fortunately, the entire Camino network is designed with the well-being of pilgrims in mind. In this section, I'll outline the resources available for staying connected and seeking help during your pilgrimage, ensuring peace of mind as you take on this spiritual adventure.

1. Important Emergency Contacts:

It's essential to have key emergency numbers at hand in case you need assistance along the Camino. Here are the most important contacts:

- Emergency Services – 112
- Fire Department – 080
- Medical Emergencies – 061
- Forest Protection – 085
- Local Police – 092
- Highway Patrol – 062
- General Reporting - 902 102 112

2. Emergency Apps:

In today's digital age, apps can be incredibly useful for ensuring your safety while walking the Camino. Here are two I've personally found helpful:

- **Pilgrim App**: Tailored for Camino de Santiago pilgrims, this app provides essential information on each stage, including distance, difficulty and points of interest such as restaurants and accommodations. You can also set alerts for any incidents and share updates with fellow pilgrims.

- **Life360**: This app allows you to track the real-time location of loved ones privately. By creating a trusted circle, you'll have the peace of mind of knowing where your family members are, which is particularly useful for those traveling solo or navigating more remote routes like the Original or Silver Way.

3. Assistance Stations Along the Route:

Strategically placed assistance points are available along the Caminos to support pilgrims in case of need. Each stage is equipped with basic amenities such as shelters, accommodation, refreshment stops and medical assistance. The managers and staff at these locations are well-trained to provide information and support in emergencies.

4. Travel Insurance:

Before starting your pilgrimage, make sure you have comprehensive travel insurance that covers medical emergencies or accidents during the Camino.

5. Pilgrim Community Support:

Don't hesitate to seek help from fellow pilgrims. The spirit of solidarity and mutual aid is a fundamental part of the Camino, and you'll find that other pilgrims are always willing to offer support and encouragement in times of need.

In summary, walking the Camino de Santiago is both a safe and rewarding experience. Though you may have initial concerns, rest assured that there are numerous resources to help ensure your safety and well-being. Stay prepared, stay informed and trust in the dedicated support network that exists for pilgrims. Walk confidently, focusing on the spiritual journey and the beauty of the landscapes you will encounter, which will remain with you for a lifetime. Now, all that's left is to enjoy your journey!

FAQ (Frequently Asked Questions)

Q: What type of adapter should I bring?
A: It's recommended to carry a type C adapter, though a type F adapter is often accepted as well. Alternatively, a universal adapter will work too.

Q: What kind of backpack should I use?
A: The ideal backpack should not exceed 40L, as the perceived weight increases with each step. A backpack between 30 and 40L, such as a 36L Osprey, is recommended.

Q: Can I bring my dog on the Camino?

A: Yes, you can! However, there are some considerations for your canine companion:

1. Dogs typically sleep 12-14 hours per day, so they may struggle to keep pace with pilgrims covering 25 km a day. Plan for more frequent rest stops.
2. Dogs are more sensitive to heat than humans, so ensure they have enough water (at least 2 extra liters per day for them). Wet their fur regularly and, if possible, avoid traveling during the hottest summer months.
3. In many regions of Spain, dogs must be kept on a leash. Additionally, wild camping is generally illegal, and not all establishments accept pets. Be sure to research and book pet-friendly accommodations such as hostels, albergues or hotels in advance.

Q: How can I relax once I arrive in Santiago de Compostela?

A: That's an easy one! Santiago offers numerous spas where you can rejuvenate and unwind. Some of my personal recommendations include:

1. Quintana Massages
2. Belmu Masajes
3. Banyen Thai Spa Urbano

DUAL PILGRIM & BONUS

Dual Pilgrim

Have you ever heard of the Dual Pilgrim program? It's a hidden treasure in the world of pilgrim age journeys.

The program began in 2015 when officials from Spain and Japan collaborated to "twin" the only two UNESCO World Heritage pilgrimage routes: the Kumano Kodo Trail in Japan and the Way of St. James/Camino de Santiago in Spain.

Recognized by UNESCO for their cultural and natural significance, these two routes offer breathtaking ways to explore well-preserved regions in their respective countries. The Dual Pilgrim program was created to honor and celebrate those who have successfully completed both of these extraordinary journeys.

BECOMING A DUAL PILGRIM

To earn the prestigious title of Dual Pilgrim, you need to complete a significant portion of both routes. There is no specific order in which the pilgrimages must be done.

For the Camino de Santiago, you must obtain the Compostela (Pilgrim's Certificate). This requires walking at least the final 100 kilometers (from Sarria to Santiago) or cycling the last 200 kilometers (with different route options) of the Camino de Santiago. Additionally, you'll need to complete one of the four designated sections of the Kumano Kodo pilgrimage in Japan.

Bonus

As a token of appreciation for reading this far, I'm offering you an additional bonus filled with the Camino de Finisterre/Muxia, practical tips for your pilgrimage (such as internet coverage, food suggestions, budget considerations and essential Spanish vocabulary), as well as details on the other route you'll need to complete to earn the Dual Pilgrim title: the Kumano Kodo. By scanning the QR code below, you'll access a brief guide for the Kumano Kodo journey. While not as detailed as this one, it provides a helpful overview of the Japanese pilgrimage route. Before I conclude, I kindly ask for one small favor:

Would you consider leaving a review on Amazon where you purchased this guide?

I know it's a minor task, but it would mean the world to me. Here's the bonus as promised; I hope you find it valuable!

Lastly, fellow pilgrim, let's end with the traditional greeting of medieval pilgrims on the Camino de Santiago:

ULTREIA!

Made in the USA
Coppell, TX
16 December 2024

42850519R00049